DATE DUE
Fecha Para Retornar

ANIMAL GEOGRAPHY

AFRICA

Joanne Mattern

Perfection Learning®

About the Author

Joanne Mattern is the author of many books for children. Her favorite topics include animals, biography, and history. She especially likes writing nonfiction because it allows her to bring real people, places, and events to life. "I firmly believe that everything in the world is a story waiting to be told."

Along with writing, Joanne enjoys speaking to school and community groups about the topics in her books. She is also a huge baseball fan and enjoys music and needlework.

Joanne lives in the Hudson Valley of New York State with her husband and young daughter. The family also includes a greyhound and two cats, and "more animals are always welcome!"

Image Credits

T = top, B = bottom, C = center, L = left, R = right

Corbis pp. 28T, 31TR, 35T, 37TR; Corel Studio pp. 6T, 9R, 14L, 14RT, 30T, 37TL, 40, 42; Gerald Cubitt pp. 49T, 50B, 52T; PhotoDisc p. 9L; Eyewire pp. 10TL, 12R, 24TL, 26TR, 27L, 34, 35R, 38TL, 52B; Chinch Gryniewicz, Ecoscene/CORBIS p. 32B; Chris Hellier/CORBIS p. 51; Peter Johnson/CORBIS p. 41; Joe McDonald/CORBIS pp. 12L, 13T; Yogi, Inc./CORBIS p. 8BR

ArtToday (www.arttoday.com) pp. 10R, 13B, 14BR; Corel pp. 3, 5, 6B, 7L, 7CR, 8L, 8TR, 11, 15, 16, 17, 18, 19, 20, 21, 22, 23, 24B, 24TR, 24CL, 25, 26C, 26B, 27R, 28B, 29, 30B, 31L, 31BR, 32T, 33, 36, 37BR, 38BL, 38R, 39, 43, 44, 45, 46, 47, 48, 49B, 50T, 54, 56; IMSI Master Photos pp. 7TR, 7BR, 10BL

Printed in the United States of America.

For information, contact

Perfection Learning® Corporation,

1000 North Second Avenue, P.O. Box 500,

Logan, Iowa 51546-0500.

Phone: 1-800-831-4190 • Fax: 1-712-644-2392

Paperback ISBN 0-7891-5331-9

Cover Craft® ISBN 0-7807-9713-2

Table of Contents

Chapter 1 The World of Africa

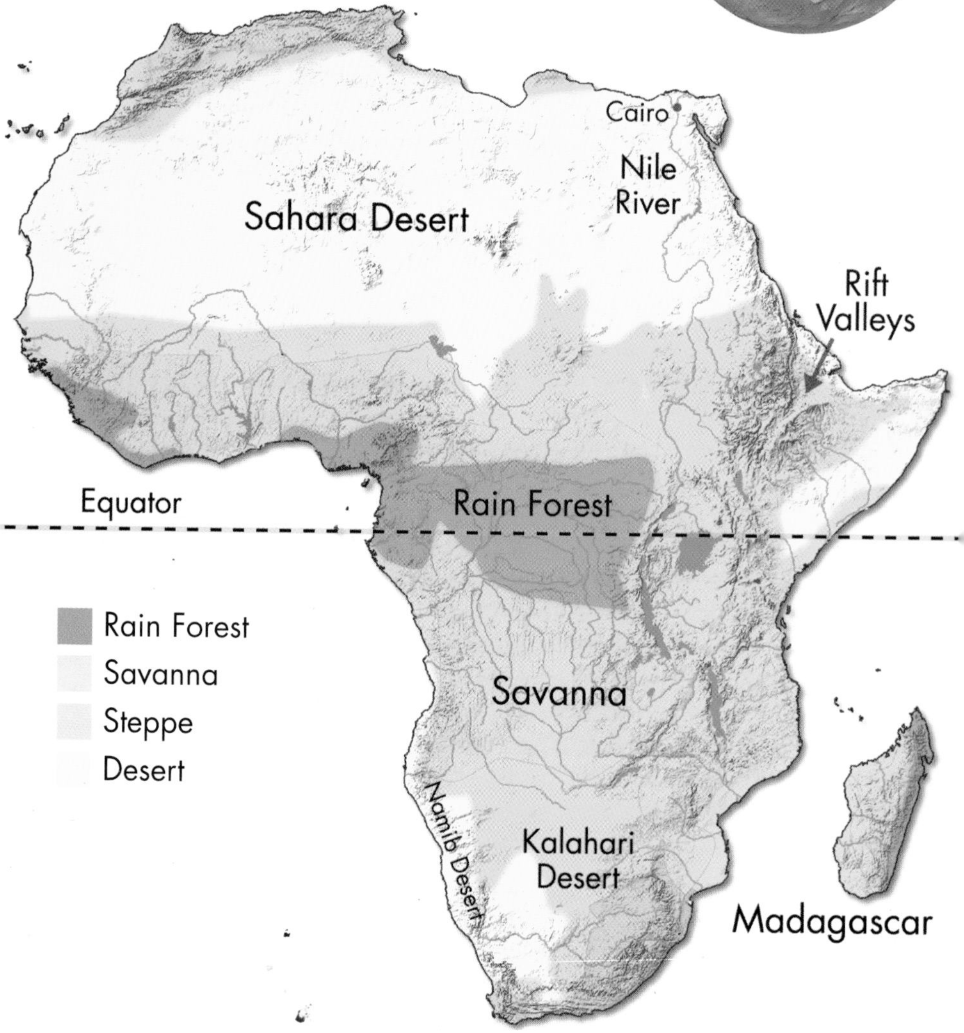

Africa is the second largest continent in the world. It covers about 11.7 million square miles. That's 22 percent of the world's total land area. And it's about four times the size of the United States. Because it is such a large continent, many different types of **habitats** can be found there.

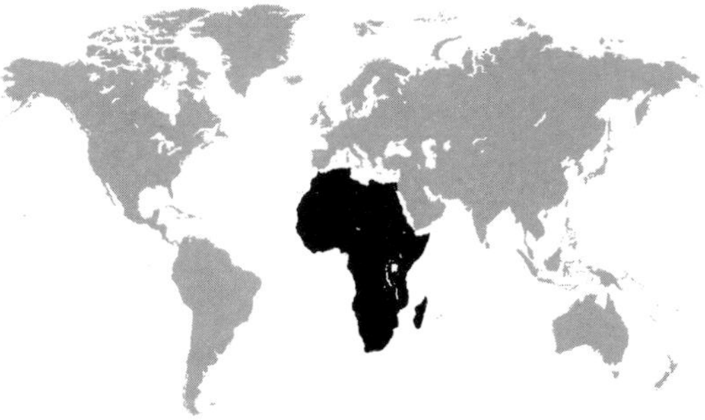

Northern and southern Africa are very hot and dry. The Sahara **Desert** covers much of northern Africa. The Kalahari and the Namib Deserts are found in southern Africa. The highest temperature ever recorded, 136°F, was in an African desert. It is not unusual for temperatures to be over 120°F daily.

Just north of Africa's southern deserts are huge areas of grassland called *savannas*. The savannas are home to large herds of grazing animals.

The central part of Africa is located on the **equator**. This part of the continent is hot and wet. Large areas of **rain forest** are found here.

In eastern Africa, there are many *rift valleys*. These valleys have flat bottoms and steep sides. Many of them contain huge lakes.

A major feature of Africa is the Nile River. The Nile is the longest river in the world. It flows for 4,145 miles. Many people live along its banks. And many animals make their homes in and near the Nile's waters.

Despite its huge size, Africa's population is relatively low. About 550 million people live in Africa. That's roughly 11.5 percent of the world's population. But that's only two times as many people as there are in the United States! The largest city, Cairo, has about 6.5 million people.

Most people live where water is available. This is along the seacoasts or the banks of the mighty Nile. Few people live in the desert because it is too hard to grow crops there.

Despite the harsh conditions on much of the continent, many different animals call Africa their home.

Chapter 2 Deserts

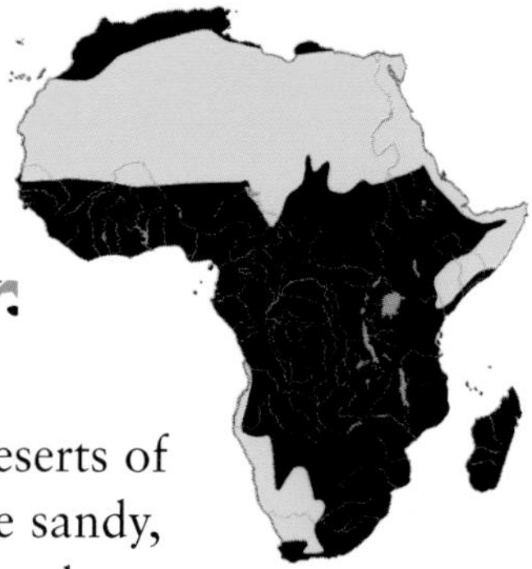

The deserts of Africa are sandy, rocky, dry places. Very little rain falls there.

The major desert of northern Africa is the Sahara. It covers 3.5 million square miles. It is the largest desert in the world.

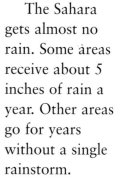

The Sahara gets almost no rain. Some areas receive about 5 inches of rain a year. Other areas go for years without a single rainstorm.

However, the Sahara does contain a number of underground rivers. These rivers often surface in places called **oases**. Oases are strong contrasts to the barren desert around them. They are "islands" of water and fertile land on the dry sand.

About one-fourth of the Sahara is shifting **sand dunes**. These dunes can reach heights of 1,400 feet! The rest of the desert is bare, rocky plains. Only a few plants grow in the Sahara. These include the date palm and the **acacia**.

How can animals survive in such harsh places? How have they **adapted** to desert habitats?

Many small animals hide underground during the day. They come out at night when it is cooler. And most desert animals can go for a long time without water. In fact, some never drink at all! Others have special body parts to help them live in the hot, dry desert. Let's meet some of the animals that call the African deserts home.

Mammals

Camel These odd-looking animals are perfectly suited for life in the dry desert. They can go without water for several weeks. How is this possible? They store fat in the humps on their backs. Fat provides energy for their bodies when food and water aren't available.

Camels have adapted for desert life in other ways too. They have long, thick eyelashes. These protect their eyes from blowing sand. Camels also are able to close their nostrils to keep out sand. And their wide feet and padded toes move easily over the sand without sinking.

continued

Camel

Camels stand about 6 feet tall at the shoulder. They are about 11 feet long.

These animals can be *domesticated*, or tamed. People who live in the desert ride camels. And they use camels to carry heavy loads.

Did You Know?

There are two kinds of camels. *Dromedary*, or Arabian, camels have only one hump. *Bactrian* camels live in China. They have two humps.

It is easy to remember which camel is which. The dromedary has one hump. So its back is shaped like the letter *D*. The bactrian has two humps. So its back is shaped like the letter *B*.

Addax Antelope Addax antelope live in some of the harshest parts of Africa's Sahara Desert. These animals never drink! They get all the moisture they need from eating plants. Their excellent sense of smell helps them find fresh grass and leaves to eat.

Addaxes live in small groups called *herds*. Their **splayed**

hooves make it easy for them to travel quickly across sand without sinking.

Addaxes are not very big. They stand about 4 feet tall at their shoulders. Their horns are almost as long—about 3.5 feet.

Many addaxes have been killed for their skins. Only a few hundred still live in the wild.

Arabian Oryx Oryx are also members of the antelope family. Their white hair reflects the heat of the desert sun. This helps them stay cool.

Unlike their cousins the addaxes, oryx do need to drink water. They find water in streams or water holes. They can even sense distant rainstorms.

Oryx will travel across the desert to find water. However, if no water is available, these animals can survive for a long time on the water found in dew and plants.

Barbary Sheep These fairly small, hoofed mammals are also perfectly suited for desert life. Barbary sheep are only about 3 feet tall at the shoulder. Their curved horns measure about 2.5 feet long.

Barbary sheep live in the mountains of the Sahara. Their hoofed feet are just right for climbing sharp rocks. Like addaxes, Barbary sheep get most of their needed water by eating plants.

Sand Cat The desert sand can get very hot. Unprotected paws would burn easily on such hot sand. But sand cats have no problem. Their paws are padded with thick fur to protect them from the scorching sand. This padding also keeps the cats from sinking into the soft sand.

Did You Know?

Like many other desert animals, sand cats aren't very big. Small animals can control their body heat better than large animals can. They also need less food and water. This is definitely an advantage when living in the desert!

Sand cats have large ears. How handy when the cats are hunting for food! These big ears can pick up faraway sounds. They help the cats locate their **prey**.

Aardwolf Aardwolves are related to hyenas. But unlike hyenas, which live in the grassy savannas, aardwolves live in the desert. They make their homes in southern Africa's Kalahari Desert.

Most hyenas are *carnivores*. This means they eat meat. But aardwolves are different. They eat insects. Their favorite food is termites.

Since their food is small and soft, aardwolves don't need strong, flat teeth to crush their prey. Their teeth are just a few small pegs.

Fennec Fox Fennec foxes have a very special feature—their ears. They are very large, up to 6 inches long.

These big ears help fennec foxes

in two ways. First, they make it easy for the foxes to hear prey.

Second, they help the foxes keep cool. How does this work? The surface of the foxes' ears are thin and full of blood vessels. The large surface area allows heat to escape from the foxes' blood into the air.

Jerboa These little animals look like mice. But they hop like kangaroos! Their huge back legs are four times as long as their front legs. They can jump up to 8 feet. This ability allows jerboas to leap away from animals, such as fennec foxes, that want to eat them. Long legs are also a good way to travel quickly across burning hot sand.

The jerboas' front legs are very short. But they come in handy too. Jerboas use them to *burrow*, or dig, into the sand. They spend the hottest part of the day in their underground homes. Then they come out at night when it is cooler.

The jerboas' bodies are only about 6 inches long. But their tails can be up to 10 inches long! These long tails provide balance when they jump. Jerboas also depend on their tails to hold them up when they're standing.

Desert Hedgehog Like many other small animals in this hot world, desert hedgehogs spend their days underground in their burrows. They come out at night to hunt.

One way hedgehogs have adapted to the desert can be seen in their legs. Their legs are long enough to hold their bodies up off the hot sand.

Desert hedgehogs eat insects. They also eat scorpions. These members of the spider family are very poisonous! But hedgehogs have learned to get around that problem. They simply bite off the stinger. Then they spit it out before they eat their crunchy meal.

Meerkat Meerkats make their homes in the Kalahari Desert and other dry parts of southern Africa. They are members of the mongoose family. These slender animals weigh about 2 pounds.

The meerkats' long, thin bodies make them good at burrowing underground. Up to 30 meerkats live in **colonies** in underground tunnels.

Several meerkats often sit at the entrances to the burrows. They are the lookouts for danger. If they see an enemy approaching, they bark sharply to warn the others. Sometimes meerkats stand up on their back legs to get a better view.

Meerkats hunt during the day. They search for insects, frogs, lizards, and eggs by turning over stones.

Meerkats are easy to tame. Some people in Africa keep them as house pets. They are great mice hunters.

Birds

Sand Grouse Unlike other desert animals, sand grouse need to drink water every day. They fly across the desert to find it. They often make round trips of more than 70 miles.

But what about the chicks that aren't old enough to fly? Adult males sit in water until their feathers are soaking wet. Then they fly back to the nests. Their chicks drink from the males' feathers.

Because the desert is so hot, sand grouse must take special care of their eggs. The birds sit on the eggs to prevent them from overheating. Sometimes the females will stand up and spread their wings. This also shades the eggs and protects them from the sun.

Sooty Falcon Sooty falcons got their name because their feathers are gray, the color of soot. These fierce hunters usually prey on small animals or birds. The falcons fly quickly after their victims. Then they kill the animals with jabs of their sharp beaks.

Sooty falcon chicks hatch late in the summer. Many other small birds **migrate** across the Sahara at this time of year. The mother and father falcons catch and kill these migrating birds. Then they feed the kill to their hungry young.

Reptiles and Amphibians

Chameleon Chameleons are some of the strangest members of the reptile family. They change colors in response to heat, light, or danger.

Chameleons eat insects. They catch their food by using their very special tongues. Their

tongues are several inches long. And they can stretch almost twice the length of their bodies. Usually, chameleons keep their tongues curled up in the back of their mouths. But when an insect flies by, they flick their tongues out so fast that they are hard to see.

Did You Know?

Like all reptiles, chameleons are *cold-blooded*. This means their body temperature is the same as the air around them. If chameleons become too hot, they will die. This is why these reptiles must find cool places to hide during the hottest part of the day.

Spiny-Tailed Agama
These members of the lizard family have tails that help them survive hard times. Agamas eat insects. But sometimes they can't find enough food. Not to worry! When food is scarce, agamas live off the fat stored in their tails. This extra energy supply means agamas can go without food for as long as a month.

The agamas' tails also help protect them against enemies. When **predators** attack, agamas dive headfirst into their burrows. Only their tails stick out. They lash their tails from side to side. Blows from the sharp spikes on their tails can really hurt. Most predators will go away and look for something easier to catch.

Insects and Spiders

Dung Beetle Dung beetles are *scavengers*. Scavengers eat decaying or dead material or other types of garbage. Dung beetles eat decaying plants as well as the waste droppings, or dung, from other desert animals.

continued

Dung Beetle

These beetles also have another interesting use for dung. They roll it into large balls. Then they lay their eggs inside the balls. When the *larvae*, or baby beetles, hatch, they feed off the dung surrounding them.

Did You Know?

The heaviest insects in the world are members of the beetle family. Goliath beetles live in Africa near the equator. These beetles get their name from their huge size. Males can be almost 4.5 inches long and weigh up to 3.5 ounces.

Obviously, dung beetles would make pretty unpleasant dinner guests. But the beetles, like all scavengers, do an important job. Eating waste materials helps keep the environment clean and healthy for other living things.

Dung beetles have hard, shiny shells. Their shells protect the beetles from predators. They also reflect sunlight, so the beetles keep cool.

Dung beetles are also called *scarab beetles.* Ancient Egyptians believed these beetles were magical and would bring good luck. They carved ornaments and jewelry in the shape of the beetles. These ornaments were called *scarabs.*

Scorpion Scorpions are only about 8 inches long. But these spiders know how to defend themselves against bigger animals.

Desert scorpions have stingers on the end of their tails. Scorpion stings are as poisonous as cobra bites! In fact, the poison in one scorpion's sting can kill a larger animal in just a few minutes.

Chapter 3 Savannas

More than one-third of the African continent is covered by savannas. These are huge, hot areas of dry grass.

Savannas get a few months of rainfall every year. During this time, the grass grows more than 6 feet high. The more rain an area gets, the taller and thicker the grass becomes.

During the rest of the year, there is no rain. The grass turns yellow. This grass is the main food for herds of animals, such as zebras, buffalo, and gazelles. This is why savannas are the only places on earth where these herds of grazing animals can be found.

Trees, such as acacias and **baobabs**, are well suited to hot, dry weather. These plants are vital links in the savannas' **food web**. Insects feed on the plants. In turn, birds and small animals prey on the insects. And large carnivores prey on the birds and smaller animals.

Mammals

African Buffalo African buffalo have been called the most dangerous land animals on earth. They are very **aggressive**. And they sometimes attack for no reason.

Adult males often fight one another to determine the strongest. The buffalo's strong bodies, heavy hooves, and 4-foot-wide horns make them deadly. In fact, one of these buffalo can even kill a lion!

African buffalo usually live near trees or by the reeds in a lake. They drink water at least once a day. One buffalo can drink as much as 9 gallons at a time!

Wildebeest Wildebeests are a type of antelope. They gather in huge herds when they migrate. As many as several thousand travel together. Wildebeests move thousands of miles across the savannas in search of fresh grass to eat.

Baby wildebeests can run a few hours after they are born. So they have no problem keeping up with the rest of the herd.

Did You Know?

Grazing animals form large herds to stay safe. Because these animals are large, it is easy for predators, such as lions and cheetahs, to spot them. A single animal is in great danger. This is especially true if it is young, old, or sick.

However, in large herds, strong members can gather around weaker members to protect them. Herds also have one or two animals that serve as lookouts. If just one animal spots danger, the whole herd gallops away.

Zebra Zebras usually live in small family groups. But they form larger herds during the dry season. Zebras will even roam savannas in mixed herds with other antelopes, especially wildebeests.

Herds are led by male zebras, or *stallions*. These stallions are often feared by predators. The males kick out at enemies with their sharp hooves. Zebra kicks can easily break predators' jaws or smash their teeth.

Just as no two people have the same fingerprints, no two zebras are striped the same. The zebras' stripes help them hide from their enemies. As zebras move in and out of the shadows of the long grass, their stripes make them hard to see.

Thomson's Gazelle Thomson's gazelles are much smaller than wildebeests or zebras. They are only about 2 feet tall at the shoulder. These animals have an interesting

continued

Thompson's Gazelle

way of dealing with predators. If they spot danger, the whole herd jumps up and down. They curve their bodies while holding their heads and legs stiff. This strange movement probably confuses enemies.

Impala Impalas are incredible jumpers. They can jump 30 feet in one leap. And they can run as fast as 50 miles an hour. In their rush to get away from danger, impalas will even jump over one another's backs.

There are two types of impala herds. *Harem herds* include females, their young, and one male leader.

Males not strong enough to lead a harem herd form *bachelor herds*. Some young males even live alone until they find harem herds to lead.

Did You Know?

Male antelopes often fight one another to decide on a leader. Usually, these fights include a lot of head banging. Two antelopes charge at each other and smash their long, curved horns together. The sound of these crashes can be heard for miles. Although this looks dangerous and painful, antelopes' horns and skulls are so strong that the animals rarely suffer any injuries from all this head bashing.

Giraffe Giraffes are the tallest animals on earth. Full-grown giraffes can be 18 feet tall. Even newborns are 6 feet tall!

Their 6- to 8-foot-long necks make it possible for them to eat leaves high in tall trees. They can find food in places other animals can't reach.

Amazingly, giraffes have the same number of bones in their necks as humans do—only seven. Obviously, a giraffe's neck bones are much bigger than a person's!

Herds of wildebeests, zebras, and even elephants often travel with giraffes. This makes a lot of sense. Giraffes have excellent eyesight and can see farther than any other large African mammal. This makes them terrific lookouts!

Giraffes can run up to 35 miles per hour and leap 6-foot-high fences. They will also kick fiercely with their sharp hooves when in danger.

But there is one time when giraffes are disadvantaged. This is when they are drinking. They are so tall that they must spread their legs wide apart and stretch their long necks down to drink. This awkward position makes it hard for giraffes to escape from predators.

Did You Know?

Unfortunately, elephants can destroy their own habitats. Each elephant eats up to 440 pounds of vegetation a day. Elephants push down trees, tear up grass, and strip bark from trees in their search for food.

A protected area in Tsavo, Kenya, was set aside for elephants. But it was destroyed by their feeding habits.

Elephants also need a lot of room to find food. This puts them in direct **competition** with Africa's growing human population.

Many elephants are killed for their ivory tusks. Their tusks are worth a lot of money.

Elephant African bush elephants are the largest land mammals alive today. The biggest one ever found weighed about 13.5 tons. One elephant's skin alone weighs about a ton!

It takes a lot of food to support such huge bodies. African elephants spend up to 16 hours a day searching for leaves and plants to eat. These elephants are strong enough to push over trees to reach the leaves on the top branches.

Elephants' trunks are their most interesting features. Small, fingerlike bumps on the ends of their trunks can pick up objects as tiny as berries.

Elephants also use their trunks to spray water over themselves to cool off. And they communicate by making loud trumpeting noises through their trunks.

Elephants are very intelligent animals. They communicate with one another using a variety of sounds.

These animals also have excellent memories. As elephants migrate, they remember where they have traveled before. They also remember places where something bad happened to them.

Elephants even feel sad when other elephants die. They will gather around the body and touch it gently with their trunks.

Rhinoceros There are two types of rhinoceroses living in Africa. They are the black rhinos and the white rhinos. Despite their names, both rhinos are actually gray.

Black rhinos have specially designed upper lips. They are shaped like hooks. The rhinos pull leaves and twigs from plants with their special lips.

They also stand on their back legs to break off tree branches with their horns. Their mouths are very tough. These rhinos can even eat the sharp thorns on acacia trees.

Black rhinos are big. They are about 12 feet long and weigh up to 2,300 pounds. But they can run 30 miles per hour over short distances.

Unfortunately, these rhinos have very bad tempers. They often charge other animals for no reason and toss them into the air with their horns.

White rhinos' mouths are shaped differently than black rhinos'. Instead of pulling leaves and twigs from trees, as black rhinos do, white rhinos graze on short grass.

White rhinos are much shier than black rhinos. They are easily frightened and usually will not attack other animals.

Rhinos don't have sweat glands. They bathe in water or roll in mud to cool off. They also have poor eyesight. But they have a fantastic sense of smell. This helps them find food and know when predators, such as lions, are headed their way.

Did You Know?

Both black and white rhinos are **endangered**. There are only about 2,500 black rhinos left in Africa. And white rhinos have been wiped out completely in some parts of the continent. Part of the reason there are so few rhinos is that they reproduce very slowly. It takes 16 months for baby rhinos to be born. And females only have one baby every three or four years.

But humans are the biggest threat. They *poach*, or kill, rhinos for their horns.

Lions are the only cats that live in groups. These groups are called *prides*. A pride of lions can include up to 30 related females, their cubs, and one male leader.

Lion Many people think lions are terribly fierce hunters. Actually, like most cats, lions spend 21 hours a day sleeping.

A group of lions can bring down an animal weighing three-quarters of a ton. And one lion can swallow up to 75 pounds of meat at one kill.

While males guard their **territories**, females hunt. They only hunt every few days. But when lions are hunting, other animals better watch out!

Cheetah Cheetahs are built for speed! Their long legs make them fast runners. Their lungs, hearts, and blood vessels are larger than those of other animals their size. They have to be large to supply plenty of oxygen to these big cats' muscles. The cheetahs' spines are flexible. This also helps them move quickly.

continued

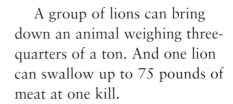

Cheetah

Unlike other cats, cheetahs cannot *retract*, or pull in, their claws. This means that cheetahs' claws dig into the ground as they run. The claws act like spikes on athletes' shoes. They grip the ground to provide traction.

All these special adaptations make cheetahs the fastest land animals. They can run more than 60 miles an hour over short distances.

In spite of their incredible speed, these animals are endangered. Cheetahs hunt only a

few animal **species**, usually gazelles or impalas. If something happens to their prey, cheetahs starve to death.

Cheetahs also do not have many cubs. And the cubs they do have often get sick. About 75 percent of cubs die before they reach 6 months of age.

Serval These long-legged cats are smaller than cheetahs. They are only about 3 feet long and 2 feet high at the shoulder. But they are also fast runners and good hunters.

Servals feed mostly on small mammals, lizards, and birds. Their long legs make them good jumpers and climbers. This helps them catch birds and other animals that live in trees.

Servals also have very big ears. These ears help them listen for small animals and lizards moving through the long grass.

These cats only weigh between 20 and 40 pounds. But they are strong enough to kill young antelopes.

They like to lie in the long grass during the hot days. At night, they hunt. It is cooler, and other animals are more active then.

Baboon These members of the monkey family live in large groups called *troops*. As many as 300 baboons live together. They travel over the ground, looking for food. A baboon eats a wide variety of things, including insects, worms, eggs, reptiles, small mammals, fruit, and plants.

Baboons are powerful, aggressive animals. But they also like to play. One baboon might jump on another's back for a piggyback ride!

continued

Baboon

These animals are also very smart. Baboons distinguish colors. And they communicate with one another through a number of cries and calls.

Did You Know?

There are many different types of baboons. The largest are the chacmas of southern Africa. They are also called *pigtailed baboons.* Adult male chacmas can weigh up to 90 pounds.

Other baboons include olive baboons, yellow baboons, North African hamadryas, and mandrills.

Warthog These animals get their name from the wartlike lumps on their faces. They are members of the wild pig family.

Warthogs are often bothered by insects and other pests. To get rid of these pests, warthogs do a lot of scratching. They also *wallow* in the mud. Rolling around in some nice, wet mud also keeps warthogs cool during the heat of the day.

Spotted Hyena Hyenas are both hunters and scavengers. These animals come out at night to hunt in groups.

Hyenas aren't that big. They're only about 5 feet long and 3 feet high at the shoulder. But one group of hyenas can kill much bigger animals, such as wildebeests or zebras. Hyenas also eat the remains of animals killed by others. Their heavy jaws and teeth are strong enough to crush bones.

These little hyenas are very fierce. A pack can chase lions away from their kill. Then the hyenas move in for the feast!

Hyenas are famous for their laugh. But they aren't really laughing. When hyenas are excited or angry, they make high, shrill cries that sound like laughs.

Did You Know?

Hyenas look like dogs. But they are actually members of the **mongoose** family.

African Hunting Dog
Members of this species are also called *wild dogs*. African hunting dogs live and hunt in large packs. As many as 60 dogs can be in a single pack. Each pack has its own territory.

Packs hunt grazing animals, such as gazelles and zebras. Working and living together help these dogs survive. Single dogs cannot catch prey by themselves. So they would die on their own.

African hunting dogs are terrific runners. These animals can run 25 miles an hour over long distances.

Jackal Jackals are members of the dog family. But they aren't hunters like the wild dogs. Instead, they are scavengers. Jackals hang around the kill of larger animals. Then they move in to eat after the larger animals have eaten and left. Jackals also find scraps of meat, vegetables, and other leftovers around people's houses.

Birds

Ostrich Ostriches, like only a few other birds, cannot fly. Their wings simply aren't strong enough to lift these big birds off the ground. But that doesn't mean they have trouble getting around.

Ostriches are great runners. Their long legs help them run up to 45 miles an hour. This is as fast as racehorses run!

Ostriches are the world's largest birds. Males grow up to 9 feet tall and weigh 345 pounds.

continued

White-backed vultures with carrion

Ostrich

Females lay the world's largest eggs. Ostrich eggs are about 6 to 8 inches long and 4 to 6 inches around. They weigh close to 4 pounds.

Ostriches are very big and fast. Therefore, they have few enemies. They are also very aggressive. They have even been known to charge trains!

These birds kick very hard. Even lions stay away from them!

White-Backed Vulture Like all vultures, these birds are scavengers. They feed on *carrion*, or the remains of dead animals. Vultures have very good eyesight. They fly high above the savannas and look for dead animals on the ground below.

Vultures have no feathers on their heads and necks. This comes in handy when the birds are feeding. Sticking their heads into the carrion can get pretty messy. Feathers would quickly become dirty and bloody. So the vultures are better off without them.

South African Crowned Crane These flashy-looking birds are sometimes called *living fossils.* This is because they are **descended** from cranes that lived millions of years ago.

Crowned cranes have long, straight beaks. These make it

possible for the cranes to eat a variety of food—everything from insects to seeds and plants.

Like all cranes, crowned cranes are good dancers. They dance to attract mates. They also dance when they are scared or excited.

Red-Headed Weaver

Weavers build very fancy nests.

The males use their beaks to weave long pieces of grass into strong, round, waterproof homes.

These birds usually hang their nests at the ends of branches. This keeps them safe from enemies. Some weaver birds' nests even have long tunnels to keep snakes out.

Thick walls protect the chicks from enemies. They also keep the chicks cool during the day and warm at night.

Insects

Termite Termites live in huge colonies inside nests called *termite mounds*. Some termite

mounds are taller than most people. The largest one ever found was 42 feet high! The outsides of the mounds are very hard. These keep predators out and maintain comfortable temperatures inside.

Termites have specific jobs to do. Queens spend their lives deep inside the mounds. They lay thousands of eggs each day.

Other termites bring decaying plants into the mounds. **Fungi** grow on these plants. The termites use the fungi for food.

Still other termites are soldiers. They have strong jaws to attack any enemies that try to harm the colony.

Chapter 4 Rain Forests and Lakes

Rain forests stretch across west and central Africa. A variety of animals lives in this wet, warm environment. There are plenty of plants and trees to provide food and homes for animals. And the warm temperatures allow cold-blooded animals, such as reptiles, amphibians, and insects, to grow quite large.

The layers of the rain forests differ from one another. The highest layer is the *canopy*. It is formed by the tops of the trees. Flying and climbing animals make their homes in the canopy's thick leaves.

Below the canopy is the *understory*, or lower canopy. This area is shaded by the taller trees. The trees here aren't as thick as they are above. Many animals move back and forth between the canopy and understory.

Finally, the lowest layer is

the *forest floor*. The floor is covered with decaying material, such as fruit and leaves that have fallen from the trees above. Millions of insects, including ants and beetles, live on the forest floor and feed on the material there. Animals that spend most of their time in the trees, such as chimpanzees and leopards, also come down to the forest floor to hunt.

Another important physical feature of the central part of Africa is the Great Rift Valley. This valley is more than 4,000 miles long and filled with many lakes. These lakes create rich habitats where animals and plants live.

Mammals

Gorilla Gorillas are the largest members of the ape family. Adult males can grow up to 6 feet tall. Some weigh three times as much as a person. Females are much smaller.

Despite their huge size, gorillas are gentle creatures. These *herbivores*, or plant eaters, feed mostly on leaves, bark, and fruit.

Gorillas live in family troops. These groups often have up to 30 members and are led by an adult male. The troops travel through the rain forest, eating plants. At night, they sleep high in the trees on platforms made of branches.

As male gorillas get older, the hair on their backs turns silver. For this reason, these gorillas are known as *silverbacks*.

Did You Know?

There are two main groups of gorillas. Mountain gorillas live in the mountain forests of east-central Africa. Lowland gorillas live farther west. Both groups are **threatened** as humans move into their habitats. Mountain gorillas have also been harmed when wars destroyed their homes.

Chimpanzee Some of the smartest animals on earth are chimpanzees. Not many animals have figured out how to use tools. But chimpanzees have!

They sometimes use sticks to dig termites out of their nests. Chimps also have been spotted using stones as hammers. Scientists have even taught the chimps to communicate with people using sign language.

Chimpanzees are at home both in the trees and on the ground. They walk along the ground on all fours. Or they swing through the trees using their long, powerful arms.

Like gorillas, chimps live in troops. Sometimes unrelated adults will form their own troops.

Chimpanzees are *omnivores*. They eat both plants and animals. Most of their diet is made up of fruit and vegetables. But they also eat insects, eggs, birds, lizards, and small mammals.

Colobus Monkey There are several types of colobus monkeys. Some are black and white and have beautiful white capes of fur on their backs. Others are red.

Like other monkeys, colobus monkeys are very good at swinging through the trees of the rain forest.

Most monkeys are omnivores. But colobus monkeys are herbivores. They only eat plants.

Leopard These cats are expert tree climbers. In fact, leopards spend most of their time in trees. They even sleep in the trees.

Leopards also drag their prey up into the trees to keep it safe from hyenas and other animals. This takes a lot of strength, because leopards prey on large animals, such as antelopes and monkeys. Leopards sometimes leap down from trees to attack their prey.

These cats often grow as long as 8 feet from nose to tail. They hunt at night. They use their excellent senses of sight and hearing to find prey. Once leopards locate prey, they creep up on it slowly and quietly. Then the leopards charge forward and attack.

Royal Antelope These tiny antelope aren't much bigger than rabbits! They are about 2 feet long and only 1 foot high at the shoulder. In fact, they are the smallest antelope in the world. Unlike their larger relatives that graze on savanna grass, royal antelope eat leaves.

Royal antelope are small, shy animals. They have very thin legs. But they can still get away from predators. Royal antelope can leap up to 9 feet in one bound.

Okapi Okapis are related to giraffes. But they are much smaller. They are only about 5 feet 6 inches tall at the shoulder. Okapis' striped legs help them blend into the trees and hide from predators such as leopards.

Trees also provide the okapis' food. They pull leaves from trees and bushes using their long tongues. Their tongues are so

continued

long, okapis can lick their eyes clean!

Okapis live in pairs or small family groups. They are some of the rarest animals in the African rain forest.

Hippopotamus These big, heavy animals are related to pigs. Hippos spend most of the day resting in lakes. In fact, they are more comfortable in the water than they are on land. Some weigh more than 2,500 pounds. So it's easier for them to swim than walk.

The water also keeps the hippos cool and moist. If hippos' skin gets too dry, they will die. They can stay underwater for up to 6 minutes.

Hippos feed at night. They use their lips and sharp teeth like lawn mowers to munch on grass and water plants. One hippo can eat up to 180 pounds of plant material in one night.

Pangolin Pangolins are covered with hard scales. They look like they are wearing suits of armor! These scales protect them from enemies.

Their bodies are only about 18 inches long. But their tails can reach 2 feet in length. Pangolins use their very strong tails like extra hands. They often hang from branches by the tips of their tails. This type of tail is called *prehensile*.

Pangolins eat termites and ants. They use their powerful front legs to tear open the nests. Then they lick up the insects with their long tongues.

Fruit Bat The rain forest is the perfect home for fruit bats. The warm, wet weather means that fruit grows all year. And since fruit is their main food, these bats have plenty to eat in the rain forest.

Fruit bats are part of a group called *megabats*. Megabats have big eyes and long noses to help them find fruit. Once they find some soft, ripe fruit, the bats mash it in their mouths. Then they swallow the juice and pulp and spit out the seeds and skin.

Birds

Jacana These long-legged birds can walk on top of floating water plants. Their long toes allow them to spread out

continued

Jacana

their weight and keep them from sinking. As they walk along, they gobble up water insects and shellfish in their long bills.

Jacanas also use the water to hide from predators. If danger approaches, they hop underwater. Only their bills show above the surface.

Hornbill Hornbills have sharp beaks. They use their beaks to cut up fruit, which is the main food of hornbills.

Hornbills also have a strange bony ridge on top of their bills. This ridge is called a *casque.* The casque helps hornbills recognize one another. These birds can tell the age, sex, and species of other hornbills just by looking at their casques.

Hornbills nest in hollow trees. When females are ready to lay their eggs, males block the

entrances to the tree holes with mud. This seals the females and their eggs inside. It's up to the males to feed their mates by passing fruit through slits in the mud. This nesting method protects the female hornbills and her chicks from predators such as monkeys and eagles.

Crowned Eagle These birds live in the tall trees at the top of the canopy. Crowned eagles build huge nesting platforms in the treetops. These platforms are big enough to hold the parents, baby birds, and any prey brought up to the nests. After the prey is eaten, the bones remain on the platforms and become part of the structures.

Eagles are fierce hunters. Big feet, strong claws, and powerful hooked beaks help the birds catch large prey such as monkeys and other birds.

Flamingo Thousands of flamingos live on the salty lakes of the Great Rift Valley. These lakes are too salty for fish and mammals. But they are perfect for flamingos.

Lesser flamingos are one type of flamingo. They eat only tiny plant life that grows in salty water. Another type, the greater flamingos, eats small shellfish and insect larvae. These flamingos live near fresh water.

Flamingos have a strange way of eating. They scoop up mud and water in their bills. Then they strain out the tiny plants and animals and squirt out the water.

Did You Know?

Flamingos aren't naturally pink. A chemical in the food they eat makes their feathers turn pink or red.

Reptiles and Amphibians

Gaboon Viper These snakes are very poisonous. The **venom** from just one snake can kill 20 people!

Their 2-inch-long fangs allow these snakes to inject their venom deep into the bodies of small animals and birds. Gaboon vipers hide among the dead leaves on the forest floor. As soon as a small animal passes

continued

Gaboon Viper

by, a viper springs forward to sink in its fangs for the kill.

Did You Know?

The patterns on gaboon vipers' bodies make them hard to see. This type of protective coloring is called *camouflage*. Camouflage helps animals in two ways. It makes it hard for predators to see the animals and attack them. And it makes it hard for the animals' prey to see them coming until it's too late.

Goliath Frog Goliath frogs are about 1 foot long. They can swallow whole mice!

The largest one ever found measured 14.5 inches. This did not include its legs, which added another 20 inches. This is a total length of 34.5 inches! And it weighed 8 pounds! These giants are the largest frogs in the world.

Goliath frogs' legs are specially designed to help these big frogs move around. Long back legs allow them to jump more than 10 feet in one leap. Short front legs help cushion the impact of landing.

Goliath frogs are also excellent swimmers. Their long back legs and webbed feet help them move quickly and easily through the water.

Mollusk

Giant African Snail

These snails are quite large. They measure up to 13 inches long. Like all snails, African snails have rough tongues that help them scrape bits of leaves from plants.

Their heads also have several **tentacles**. Two of these are long and have simple eyes at the end. These eyes don't see very well. In fact, about all they can do is tell light from dark. The other tentacles are used for smelling and feeling.

The snails' bodies are very soft and moist. But they are protected by hard shells on the snails' backs. When predators threaten the snails, they pull their bodies into their shells and hide until the danger passes. The shells are also good places for snails to stay when the weather is very hot or very dry.

Chapter 5 Rivers

The Nile is the most important river in Africa. It begins in Tanzania in eastern Africa. From there, it takes a winding course northward until it empties into the Mediterranean Sea. The Nile is the longest river in the world. Its many **tributaries** provide vital sources of water for Africa's people, animals, and plants.

There are other rivers in Africa besides the Nile. Some of the more important ones are the Niger River in the west, the Congo River in central Africa, and the Zambezi River in the southern part of the continent.

Rivers are not the same all along their length. In some parts, the water is cool and clear and moves very fast. Fish and other animals that live in these parts of the river must be good swimmers. If not, the currents will sweep them away.

Other parts of the rivers are slow, deep, and broad. These parts are usually muddy and warm. Many animals live in these quieter parts of the river.

Because Africa is a warm continent, its rivers are full of life. Africa's rivers are home to a large variety of small fish

including knife fish, cichlids, and yellow fish. Insects, reptiles, amphibians, and birds also find plenty to eat and drink along the banks of Africa's rivers.

Fish

Nile Perch Nile perch are among the largest freshwater fish on earth. They weigh more than people. These fish are fierce predators. They feed on the smaller fish that swim in the Nile.

Lungfish Most fish don't breathe air. But the lungfish do! These fish have gills, but they don't often use them. Instead, lungfish breathe air through special lungs. Therefore, these fish must rise to the surface of the water to breathe.

Lungfish are different from other fish in another way. They *estivate*, or become inactive, during dry periods.

During the dry season, they burrow into the mud and curl into tight balls. Then they secrete mucus to cover their bodies. The mud sticks to the mucus and forms hard cases that protect the fish. Only a small hole remains for the lungfish to breathe through.

The cases soften when they get wet. Then the lungfish emerge and swim away. Lungfish usually estivate for just a few months. But some have been known to estivate for several years.

Did You Know?

Lungfish are descended from a group of air-breathing fish that lived during the Paleozoic era. That was more than 225 million years ago!

Birds

Osprey Ospreys eat fish that they snatch from the water. Their long, sharp claws grab slippery, moving fish. Adult ospreys can carry a 4-pound fish. This is more than the birds themselves weigh.

Some ospreys live in Europe. But when fall comes and the weather gets cold, these birds migrate to Africa. It's warmer there, and food is plentiful.

Kingfisher These birds also swoop down on fish from the air. They wait on low

branches and watch the water. When they see fish, they dive close to the water and scoop the fish up in their pointed beaks. Then they toss the fish up in the air and swallow them headfirst.

Kingfishers have big appetites. The parents bring fish back to their nests for their chicks to eat. Young kingfishers can eat more than 15 fish a day.

Heron Like ospreys and kingfishers, herons are good at catching fish. But they don't catch them from the air. Instead, these 5-foot-tall birds stand in the shallow water or on the bank. They stare into the water, looking for fish. Then they lean down and grab the fish in their long, sharp bills.

continued

Heron

Herons live in large colonies. They build their nests in low trees or bushes.

Reptile

Nile Crocodile

There are many kinds of crocodiles in the world. But Nile crocodiles are probably the most dangerous to people. These huge reptiles can

grow to 16 feet long. They have killed more people than any other animal in Africa.

Crocodiles are perfectly designed for hunting. They have sharp eyesight, good hearing, and an excellent sense of smell. All these senses help crocodiles find their prey. Crocodiles mainly dine on fish. But they also eat any animal they can drag into the water.

Insect

Dragonfly These fierce killers prey on smaller insects. Dragonflies hold their legs underneath them and catch other insects as they fly.

Dragonflies lay their eggs in water. A few weeks later, the young, called *nymphs*, hatch. Nymphs have no wings. They live in water for up to 5 years while their bodies develop into adults.

Nymphs can be quite fierce as they hunt smaller insects in the water. Yet, they are also eaten by fish, birds, and other river animals.

Crustacean

Freshwater Shrimp
These tiny creatures might be the most important creatures in the river. They are the main food for most fish and insects. Fish and insects, in turn, are eaten by larger animals, such as birds and reptiles. So shrimps are the backbone of the river's food web.

Even though they are food for many other creatures, shrimps have to eat too! These little creatures feed on microscopic plants. They filter these plants out of the water with their front legs.

Chapter 6 Madagascar

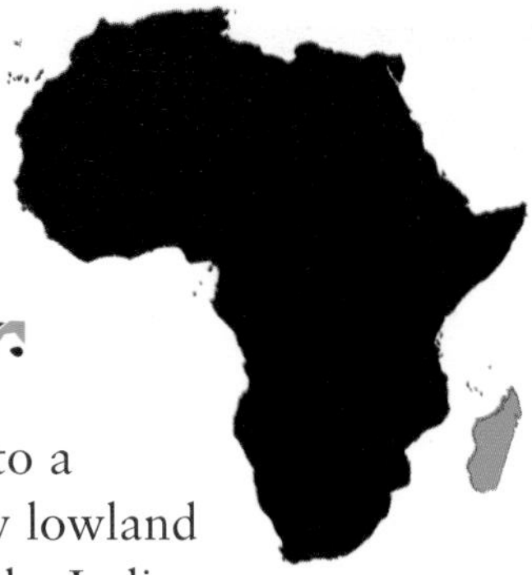

Madagascar is a very special place. Today it is the fourth largest island in the world. But millions of years ago, Madagascar was connected to Africa.

Madagascar covers 226,658 square miles. It is just a little smaller than Texas. The central part of the island is a mountainous **plateau** which rises as high as 9,436 feet in the northern part of the country. There are several river valleys in this plateau. The land slopes down to a narrow lowland along the Indian Ocean in the east and a wider coastal plain in the west.

The eastern part of Madagascar borders the Indian Ocean and gets a lot of rain. Up to 120 inches fall a year. The central part of the island is drier. And the southern and southwestern areas are very dry. They get only about 15 inches of rain a year.

Baobab grove

The great variety of rainfall leads to a variety of habitats. Eastern Madagascar is covered with rain forests. And the western part of the island is made up of savannas. The dry south and southwest are deserts.

The ancestors of Madagascar's animals originally came from Africa. But Madagascar has been separated from the continent for a very long time. Therefore, the animals there are different from the animals in Africa. In fact, nine out of ten of Madagascar's animal species aren't found anywhere else in the world. For example, Madagascar is the only place where mammals such as the lemur and the tenrec are found. Let's find out more about Madagascar's unusual animal residents.

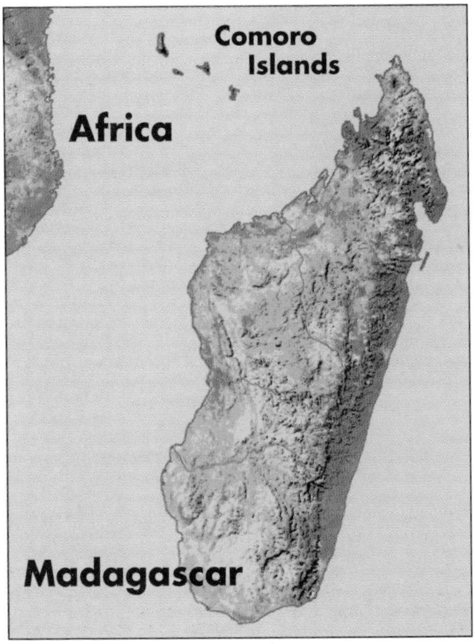

Mammals

Ring-Tailed Lemur

These animals are very sociable. They live in family groups of up to 40 members. They are also very territorial. Ring-tailed lemurs mark their territories with a chemical made in scent glands on their bodies. The scent tells other lemurs to stay out!

It's easy to see how ring-tailed lemurs got their name. Their bodies are 18 inches long. But their ringed tails are about 22 inches long.

Did You Know?

Lemurs are related to monkeys. These animals have thick, furry coats, large eyes, and long **muzzles**. Many also have long, bushy tails. All lemurs live in trees and eat fruit, flowers, and leaves.

Aye-aye Aye-ayes are another type of lemur. While most lemurs live on plants, aye-ayes also eat insects. Their big ears help them hear insects moving under tree bark. Then they use their long middle fingers to pull the insects from the bark.

Aye-ayes spend most of their time in trees. Ridged pads on the bottoms of their feet help them walk along the branches.

Sifaka Sifakas get their name from the sound they make to warn other sifakas of danger. Their call sounds like "Shi-fakh! Shi-fakh!"

Their bodies are about 18 inches long. And they have 21-inch-long tails. Their legs are much longer than their arms. This lets sifakas leap more than 16 feet through the trees. Sometimes, they come down out of the trees and walk along the ground. But unlike most mammals, they must walk upright. Their arms are too short to reach the ground.

Indri Indris are the largest lemurs. They are also the noisiest! Indris make loud wailing noises that can be heard up to 2 miles away. A group of indris will make these calls to keep other indris away. Indris can also identify one another by listening to the calls.

Unlike ring-tailed lemurs, indris have short, stubby tails. But like other lemurs, indris have big eyes. These eyes help them see well in dim light. This comes in handy because lemurs are *nocturnal*, or active at night.

Perinet Natural Reserve, Madagascar

Tenrec Female tenrecs hold the record for producing the largest **litters** of any mammal. They have up to 31 babies at one time!

Tenrecs have no tails. They do have coats of stiff hair and spines. To frighten enemies, tenrecs raise the spines and hair on their heads and backs, stamp their feet, open their mouths wide, and hiss. This is pretty aggressive for an animal that is just 15 inches long!

Fossa These catlike animals prey on tenrecs, lemurs, birds, reptiles, and insects. Fossas are small—only about 2.5 feet long, not counting their tails. But they are fierce!

They catch their prey in their front paws. Then they kill their victims with a

Fossa

bite on the back of their heads. Fossas are the most common meat-eating animals on Madagascar. There are no cats or dogs on the island. So these animals have little competition for food.

Fossas' tails are almost as long as their bodies. This helps the animals balance when they are climbing trees.

Bush Pig These animals are also called *wild boars*. Bush pigs have an excellent sense of smell. They use their long noses to find roots, insects, and worms under the ground. But bush pigs aren't picky eaters. In fact, they will eat almost anything from plants to birds to dead animals. Unfortunately, bush pigs also cause a lot of damage to crops. Therefore, they are often hunted by farmers.

Birds

Wattled False Sunbird These birds have a name that is almost bigger than they are! Wattled false sunbirds are only about 4 inches long. Their long, curved beaks reach nectar deep inside flowers. Then the sunbirds curl their tongues into straws and suck up the sweet juice.

Sunbirds are important because they help **pollinate** plants. As they fly from one flower to another, they carry pollen with them.

Male sunbirds have special tricks to attract females during mating season. They develop blue skin on the sides of their heads. This really gets the females' attention!

Coral-Billed Nuthatch Vanga These are also little birds with a big name! They are only 5 inches long. They are part of a group of birds called *vanga shrikes*. These birds are found only on Madagascar.

Nuthatch vangas live in the

continued

rain forest. They use their sharp claws to cling to tree trunks. Meanwhile, they poke their sharp bills into the bark. They're looking for insects to eat.

Reptile

Parson's Chameleon

These chameleons have unusual feet. Two of their toes are opposite the other three toes. These allow the chameleons to hold tightly to branches and plants.

Chameleons' eyes are shaped like cones. Each eye can move by itself. This means chameleons can look at two things at the same time!

Did You Know?

Madagascar is the home of three-quarters of the world's species of chameleons.

Insect

Stick Insect There are about 80 different kinds of stick insects on Madagascar. None of them are found anywhere else in the world.

Stick insects can stay very still for a long time. Their long, thin bodies look so much like sticks that they are very hard to see against trees. What perfect camouflage!

Glossary

acacia shrub or tree found in warm areas; has white or yellow flowers

adapt to change in order to live under specific conditions

aggressive relating to a fierce or threatening manner

baobab broad-trunked tropical tree; edible fruit; bark used for paper, cloth, and rope

colony group that lives together

competition situation where two creatures are trying to get the same thing, such as food

descend to come from

desert area of very dry land

endangered close to extinction or dying out

equator imaginary line around the middle of the earth where the climate is very hot

food web links between eaters and what is eaten in an ecological community

fossil preserved remains of an animal or plant from millions of years ago

fungus parasitic, spore-producing organism that doesn't have chlorophyll, such as molds, rust, mildews, smuts, mushrooms, and yeasts

habitat place where animals and plants live

litter group of mammals born at the same time to one mother

migrate	to travel from one area to another
mongoose	agile, ferret-sized mammal that feeds on small animals and fruit
muzzle	animal's nose, mouth, and jaws
oasis	place in the desert where there is water. Plants and trees are able to grow.
plateau	high, flat area of land
pollinate	to carry pollen from one flower to another, causing fertilization
predator	animal that hunts other animals for food
prey	animal that is hunted by another animal for food
rain forest	thick tropical forest that is hot and humid. Usually rain occurs daily.
sand dune	large pile of drifting sand
species	a distinct type of animal or plant
splayed	spread out
tentacle	long, flexible limb of an animal used for moving, feeling, and grasping
territory	area where an animal lives
threatened	having an uncertain chance of continued survival; likely to become extinct
tributary	stream or river that flows into a larger stream or river
venom	poison produced by some snakes and other animals

Index